CHRISTMAS PROGRAMS
FOR CHILDREN

Compiled by

ELAINA MEYERS

Standard®
PUBLISHING
Bringing The Word to Life

Cincinnati, Ohio

Published by Standard Publishing

Cincinnati, Ohio

Copyright © 2007 by Standard Publishing.

All rights reserved.

ISBN 978-0-7847-1941-1

CONTENTS

BABY JESUS IS MISSING

Dixie Phillips

Summary: The Brown family is so caught up in the trappings of Christmas that they don't realize the very reason for Christmas, baby Jesus, is missing.

Characters:
JON—father of the Brown family
JENNY—mother of the Brown family
TITUS—oldest son of the Brown family
TRINITY—oldest daughter of the Brown family
JOSIAH—second child of the Brown family
ADDI—baby of the Brown family
Setting: living room
Props: Christmas tree, decorations, lots of presents, phone, nativity set, crate with Christmas lights

Scene opens with children and parents decorating the tree.

JENNY: Jon, you should see the Sylvester's tree. They have purchased all new ornaments. I bet they have over a thousand dollars invested in ornaments.
JON: Well, what's good enough for the Sylvesters is good enough for the Browns. We can't be outdone by our neighbors, now can we? Just what could we do to beat them?
ADDI: *[setting up nativity set]* Mommy, baby Jesus is missing.
JENNY: *[brushing her off]* Oh, Addi, we will worry about that later. Right now, I've got bigger fish to fry. You know what

we could do, Jon. We could buy more Christmas lights and decorate our yard with lots of beautiful decorations. That way we wouldn't be the only ones that would know that we beat those Sylvesters.

JON: Jenny, that is absolutely brilliant! While the Sylvesters' tree might have all those fancy ornaments, hardly anyone will know, but everyone who drives by our yard and the Sylvesters' will see that the Brown family celebrates Christmas in style.

TRINITY: [looks at nativity set] Daddy, baby Jesus is missing.

JON: Yes, Trinity, we'll find baby Jesus later. Right now Daddy has to get busy and put up some Christmas lights. Let the games begin!

[Phone rings.]

JENNY: [answers phone] Yes, hello, Pastor Wilkens. Oh yes, we are having a wonderful Christmas. Oh, you need someone to help at the homeless shelter? Tonight?

[JON shakes head, gesturing "no way."]

JENNY: [repeating everything the pastor says] Oh, Mrs. Clay was scheduled to help, but she came down with pneumonia.

JOSIAH: [looking at nativity set and then goes to his mother] Mommy, baby Jesus is missing!

JENNY: [holding phone away from ear] Josiah, not right now. I have a very important phone call from Pastor Wilkens. [loudly] You know what we have always taught you children: it's more blessed to get than to . . . I mean, give than to receive. . . . Forgive me, Pastor Wilkens. Little Josiah just needed my attention for a minute, and you know how important my children are to me, as a godly mother. What were you saying? [pause] Oh yes, you needed someone to fill in for Mrs. Clay at the homeless shelter this evening because she has pneumonia.

[JON jumps up and down, motioning "no way."]

JENNY: Oh, Pastor Wilkens, we would fill in for Mrs. Clay, but we have other very important plans for this evening. We are just getting our Christmas decorations out, and the children are setting up the nativity scene. It's kind of our *family* night tonight.

[JON gives JENNY the thumbs up, nodding his head up and down.]

TITUS: *[looking over nativity scene, moves towards JENNY and tugs on her dress]* Mommy! Mommy!

JENNY: Excuse me, Pastor Wilkens! Titus needs me. *[holds phone away from shoulder, glaring at TITUS]* Titus, what is so important that you would interrupt my phone call with Pastor Wilkens?

TITUS: Mommy, baby Jesus is missing.

JENNY: I'll help you find baby Jesus later. Go sit by your brother and sisters. *[goes back to chatting with Pastor Wilkens]* I'm so sorry about that, Pastor Wilkens, but little Titus and the other children can't seem to find baby Jesus. He seems to be missing from their favorite nativity set. So, you know what we will be doing tonight. . . . That's right! We'll be trying to find baby Jesus. . . . What did you say, Pastor? . . . What do you mean, "That will preach"? . . . Oh, you mean that there are so many people wrapped up in their own lives that baby Jesus is missing. They have become so selfish and trying to outdo the Sylvesters, I mean the Joneses, that they completely have missed out on the true meaning of Christmas. Baby Jesus is missing from their lives.

[JON looks at lights and starts putting them away.]

JENNY: You say that Titus has just given you your message for Sunday? Well, I'd say the children have all given Jon and me something to think about this Christmas. I guess it's like you say, Pastor Wilkens, a little child shall lead them. Say, . . . about that homeless shelter, . . . I think we can rearrange our schedules a bit and fill in for dear Mrs. Clay. What time should we be there? . . . Around five? You can count on us, Pastor Wilkens. Good-bye. See you Sunday.

CHILDREN: *[squealing with delight]* Mommy! Daddy! Look! We found baby Jesus!

[TITUS holds up figurine.]

JON: We sure did find baby Jesus.

JENNY: And let's never lose Him again.

TITUS: *[holding up baby Jesus]* Mommy, Pastor Wilkens always says we need to give a little Jesus to someone who is in need.

JOSIAH: Do you think we should give baby Jesus to someone at the homeless shelter?

JENNY: *[gathering children around parents]* No, I think we will put our baby Jesus with Mary and Joseph. *[putting figurine in place]* But we can give a little of Jesus' love to those who are hurting.

JON: *[holds crate up]* Now let's take some of our Christmas decorations to the homeless shelter and see if we can bring a little of Jesus' love to them.

TRINITY: I'm so glad we found baby Jesus!

JENNY: Me too!

[Blackout.]

S-A-M-T-S-I-R-H-C Y-R-R-E-M

Dixie Phillips

Fourteen children enter carrying poster boards
on which letters have been written.
All children hold their letters to their sides until the end
when they show the letters for the congregation to read.

UNISON: We have a little letter game we'd like to play with you.
Let the fun begin with a few important clues.

[Child holding the poster board
with the letter S and star on it says:]
S is for the star that shone that holy night.
I'm sure that it was glowing very, very bright.

[Child in a donkey costume says:]
A is for the animals that were in the stall.
I'm sure there must have been a donkey saying, "*Hee-haw!*"

[Girl dressed as Mary says:]
M is for Mary. She loved her tiny son.
An angel had told her she was the chosen one.

[Child carrying a stop sign says:]
T is for the traffic that showed up that holy night.
Many stopped to worship Him. It was quite a sight.

[Child dressed as a shepherd says:]
S is for the shepherds who left their flock of sheep,
so they could bow before Him and worship at His feet.

[Child with sign which reads "I = ME" says:]
I is for simply little old me.
I'm the one He loves for all eternity.

[Child dressed as an angel says:]
R is for rejoicing. That's what the angels did.
It sounded heavenly and quite splendid.

[Child sits on a bale of hay and says:]
H is for the hay that filled the lowly manger.
The tiny King who lay there would be a life-changer.

[Child dressed like a mouse says:]
C is for the critters that were hiding in the stall.
I'm sure there was a mouse—the tiniest critter of all.

[Child points at congregation and then at self and says:]
Y is for you and you and you and you!
Unto you a Savior's born, and unto me too!

[Child dressed like an angel points at congregation and says:]
R is for the reason why our Savior came to earth.
You're the reason why angels sang of His birth.

[Child dressed as a wise man says:]
R is for the rich gifts that the wise men brought,
To the tiny baby for days they had sought.

S-A-M-T-S-I-R-H-C Y-R-R-E-M

[Child waves at congregation and says:]
E is for everyone Jesus came to save.
If you belong to Him, let me see you wave.

[Child holding the M sign says:]
M is for the many who believe upon God's Son.
He didn't come for some. He came for *everyone*.

UNISON: The time has come to solve our Christmas mystery.
We hope you weren't too confused by the letters you did see.
And what's the Christmas message for each one today?
Merry Christmas to all! Thanks for coming to our play.

[Children in unison hold up their letters to reveal "Merry Christmas."]

THE NIGHT THE KING SLEPT IN A STABLE

Elaine Ingalls Hogg

Summary: An earthly king learns of a heavenly King and is asked to make a response to Him.
Characters:
EMPEROR AUGUSTUS
FIRST SERVANT
SECOND SERVANT—a younger boy
SERVANTS—nonspeaking parts
Setting: a room in the emperor's palace—the furniture is patched and shabby in appearance and the wallpaper is hanging off the wall
Props: throne, table, shabby robe for the emperor, one velvet trimmed robe with fur and gold braid, mirror, feather duster, treasure chest, colored gem or two, coins and paper money stored in the treasure chest, scroll for the decree, stemmed glasses, candles, fine dinnerware
Running Time: 12–15 minutes

SCENE ONE
EMPEROR AUGUSTUS wanders around the room, touching the patched furniture and pointing out the run-down state of his palace.

EMPEROR AUGUSTUS: Look at this! No man in my position should have to live like this! It's no better than a pigpen! Since when does an emperor, the most important person in the land, live in a dump and wear shabby clothes? Look at me! There's not a speck of gold trim anywhere. An important person like me should have gold on his clothes.

FIRST SERVANT: [rubbing his hands together in a nervous motion] Sir, I agree! You do need to remodel this place, and you definitely need to buy more clothes!

EMPEROR AUGUSTUS: [to his servant] Find my treasure chest and bring it to me right away. I'm going to order new clothes—fine velvet robes trimmed with furs and gold—more gold than any other leader in the world.

[FIRST SERVANT hurries out of the room and returns with the treasure chest. EMPEROR AUGUSTUS takes the chest and empties the contents on the table. Slowly he counts his money—piling it into neat stacks on the table. When he is finished counting, he shakes his head.]

FIRST SERVANT: Is there a problem?

EMPEROR AUGUSTUS: Is there a problem? Of course, there's a problem! There isn't enough money here to buy Dick Whittington's cat a new pair of boots, let alone renovate this place or build a bigger palace. There isn't even enough money to buy one new suit, let alone one trimmed in gold.

THE NIGHT THE KING SLEPT IN A STABLE

An important emperor like me needs at least 20 new suits trimmed with gold. *[He thrusts the coins and money back in the chest, slams the lid, and stands to his feet.]* I need more money! *[He paces around the room, rubs his brow as if thinking.]* I know what I'll do. Bring me my pen and a scroll! I'll tell everyone in my kingdom to go to the town where he was born and write his name in the scroll there.

FIRST SERVANT: But sir, some of the people will have to travel for days to add their names to a scroll.

EMPEROR AUGUSTUS: *[laughs out loud]* Don't you think I know that? But I'm the boss, and I'm telling them to come to the town of their births and add their names to my scroll. That is that!

[EMPEROR AUGUSTUS stomps towards the door as if to go out of the room. When he reaches the door, he stops and orders FIRST SERVANT to fetch all the other servants in the palace. FIRST SERVANT scurries out, bowing and hustling. EMPEROR AUGUSTUS circles the room and settles himself in his throne. When FIRST SERVANT returns, he has several other servants with him.]

EMPEROR AUGUSTUS: Listen to my instructions! I have an important message I want to send out to my subjects. Tomorrow morning you will go to all towns and villages in the land and take this message. Put up signs saying, "Emperor Augustus has declared that every family must go to the town where they were born and put their names in the big book there." They think I want to count them but what I really want to do is get their addresses, and then I can send them a big tax bill. *[rubs his hands in glee]* When I get all that money, I'll be the richest man on earth. Soon I'll have the nicest clothes and the biggest palace in all the land.

SCENE TWO

EMPEROR AUGUSTUS is eating his dinner and SECOND SERVANT comes up to him.

SECOND SERVANT: Excuse me, sir. I have news for you.

EMPEROR AUGUSTUS: Who has been teaching you your manners? *[roars at the little one. SECOND SERVANT trembles but stays near the table.]*

SECOND SERVANT: But this is very important, sir!

EMPEROR AUGUSTUS: I'm eating my dinner. If it isn't serious, I'll see you get a flogging.

SECOND SERVANT: It is serious, sir! Very serious! I have heard some news and I'm sure you want to hear it too.

EMPEROR AUGUSTUS: News, you say? Do tell!

[EMPEROR AUGUSTUS slams his fork on table, wipes face with napkin, and stands directly in front of SECOND SERVANT but SECOND SERVANT doesn't back away.]

SECOND SERVANT: You always say you are the most important person in the whole land, but I heard someone say that you aren't as important as you think you are.

[EMPEROR AUGUSTUS's face turns red, and he wipes his face with his napkin. He stands up as tall as he can stand.]

EMPEROR AUGUSTUS: *[in a loud voice]* Who in his right mind would ever say I'm not the most important person in these parts, if not the whole world?

SECOND SERVANT: Shepherds, sir. Some shepherds were getting water for their sheep this morning, and they said that you aren't as important as you think you are!

EMPEROR AUGUSTUS: *[laughs uproariously]* Shepherds!

Servant boy, who do you think you are talking to?

SECOND SERVANT: Sir, the shepherds said they were tending their sheep in a field near the town of Bethlehem. All at once the sky lit up with a strange light. They were so scared that they hid behind some bushes near the stream. Then they heard a noise in the sky. When they dared to look up at the sky, they saw a choir of angels. The angels were saying, "Glory to God in the highest, and on earth peace to men on whom his favor rests."

EMPEROR AUGUSTUS: Hmm! Shepherds! Angels! That must have been one outstanding party or else they were dreaming. Everyone knows that all the shepherds in the world aren't as important as an emperor. Go away and don't bother me. I'm busy. *[waves his hand in a signal of dismissal]*

SECOND SERVANT: *[backs away as if to leave and then decides against it]* But sir, the angel said the only Son of the one true God was born last night in Bethlehem.

EMPEROR AUGUSTUS: Where? There are no palaces in Bethlehem. It's the smallest town in Judah!

SECOND SERVANT: The baby wasn't born in a palace. He wasn't born in a hotel either. The innkeeper said they were all booked up.

EMPEROR AUGUSTUS: Huh! Where was He born? A barn?

THE NIGHT THE KING SLEPT IN A STABLE

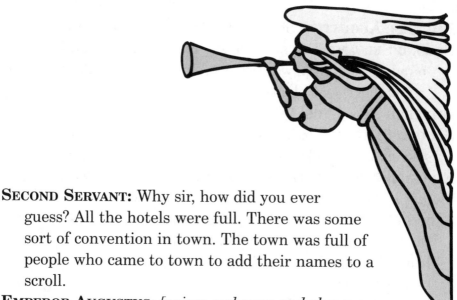

SECOND SERVANT: Why sir, how did you ever guess? All the hotels were full. There was some sort of convention in town. The town was full of people who came to town to add their names to a scroll.

EMPEROR AUGUSTUS: *[raises eyebrows and shows a little more interest in what the servant is telling him]* How did the shepherds know where to find this baby?

SECOND SERVANT: The angel gave them a sign so they would know which baby was God's Son.

EMPEROR AUGUSTUS: *[laughs]* Ha! A sign! Did someone paint a sign and put it in front of the barn saying "God's Son Was Born Here"? Is this some kind of joke?

SECOND SERVANT: No sir, no sir, no joke. The angel said, "This will be a sign to you: You will find a baby wrapped in cloths and lying in a manger."

EMPEROR AUGUSTUS: *[wanders around the room and then climbs onto his throne]* God would never allow His Son to be born in a barn. No one would put strips of cloth on a king! They would only wrap the Son of God in linen or silk. This is a foolish story. Why, God would only invite kings and queens and emperors to the birth of His Son. People like me.

SECOND SERVANT: *[crossing the room and standing in front of the throne]* That's not what the shepherds said.

THE NIGHT THE KING SLEPT IN A STABLE

EMPEROR AUGUSTUS: Shepherds! Phooey on shepherds!

SECOND SERVANT: But sir! The shepherds have proof! They found the baby. He was wrapped in strips of cloth and lying in a manger, just like the angels had said.

EMPEROR AUGUSTUS: What nonsense!

SECOND SERVANT: *[in a hesitant manner]* Sir, the shepherds said something else too.

EMPEROR AUGUSTUS: *[lets us know he is agitated by the tone of his voice]* What? What did they say?

SECOND SERVANT: Your Honor, the ancient Scriptures say He is the Son of God. Besides, not even King Herod had angels singing when he was born.

EMPEROR AUGUSTUS: The very idea! The Son of God . . . born in a barn . . . in Bethlehem? Impossible!

[Then EMPEROR AUGUSTUS drops his head in his hands as if to think about what he has heard. Finally he looks up and he says to his servant:] What do the Holy Scriptures say?

SECOND SERVANT: A long time ago the prophet Micah wrote that even though Bethlehem was the smallest clan it was going to be the birthplace of someone who will be ruler over Israel. *[after a slight pause, SECOND SERVANT looks up at EMPEROR AUGUSTUS and says,]* Sir I believe the shepherds and the Holy Scriptures. Last night there was no room at the inn so the King of kings slept in a stable. Sir, are you more generous than the innkeeper? Will you make room for the King of kings?

[Blackout.]

THE NIGHT THE KING SLEPT IN A STABLE

I AM

Karen Leet

Summary: This is a performance poem that may be read or recited as a group or with individual assigned parts. Costumes and motions may be added.

I am the shepherds,
  dozing in a field,
  huddled by a fire,
  watching over the sheep
  this dark and silent night.

I am the angels,
  singing with great joy,
  wonderful good news
  to bring for all
  who can hear our voices.

I am the curious cattle,
  hearing a baby cry
  in our stable.
  He's cradled in straw
  and swaddling clothes.

I am Joseph
  standing watch over
  my small family—
  my beloved Mary
  and this precious baby.

I am Mary
 with this child
 in my arms,
 this amazing baby,
 this gift from God.

I am the star,
 bright-lighting the sky,
 leading the way
 to a quiet stable
 and one small baby there.

I am this night of nights,
 this miracle moment,
 this wonder of wonder,
 this time when God
 sends His Son to a stable.

I am me, and I am filled
 with joy and praise and
 hope and thankfulness
 to think of Jesus, born
 in Bethlehem—a gift for me!

I AM

NO ROOM

Karen Leet

Summary: This is a performance poem that may be read or recited as a group or with individuals assigned parts. Costumes and motions may be added.

No room, no room,
no room at all.
Go find a corner in
a stable stall.

Joseph and Mary
turned away.
Don't bother to try
another day.

No room, no room,
no room at all.
Go find a corner in
a stable stall.

Have that baby
some other place.
Too crowded here.
We have no space.

No room, no room,
no room at all.
Go find a corner in
a stable stall.

Baby born in
stable hay.
Busy innkeeper turned
them away.

NO ROOM

No room, no room,
no room at all.
Go find a corner in
a stable stall.

Baby Jesus here's
what I say,
Come to my house.
You can stay.

There's plenty of room.
I'll do my part.
You can live
inside my heart.

There's room, there's room,
there's room after all.
No need to find
a stable stall.

NO ROOM

THE LEGEND OF THE CHRISTMAS SPIDER

Amy Houts

A spider spun a spider's web
upon a Christmas tree.
"This is my gift, my humble gift,
I give for you, from me."
It shimmered and it glistened,
the spider's glossy shroud.
The children looked in wonder.
The tree stood tall and proud.
Did you know the tinsel
we place so carefully
came from the sparkling spider's web
that clothed the Christmas tree?

THEODORE'S STARRY NIGHT

Jody A. Ingalls

Summary: A lonely rabbit finds love and a home as he witnesses the birth of the Savior.

Characters/Puppets:

THEODORE—a lonely rabbit looking for a home

CAT—an outgoing cat belonging to Mary and Joseph

MOUSE—the cat's squeaky-voiced and timid friend

AL—an energetic alligator who keeps popping up in the wrong story

SHEEP—a lamb who hears Christ's birth announcement by the angels

COW—a resident of the Christmas stable

HEN—a resident of the Christmas stable

ROOSTER—a resident of the Christmas stable

GOAT—a resident of the Christmas stable

[The last four puppets can be changed or combined as needed.]

Setting: Bethlehem, the night of the first Christmas

Props: puppets and puppet stage

Also needed: children's choir and soloist (If these are not available, the listed songs may be sung by the congregation. Other appropriate songs may be substituted for those included with the program as needed.)

Running Time: approximately 30 minutes (depends on the songs used)

SCENE ONE: a field outside of Bethlehem

THEODORE enters, alone and shivering.

THEODORE: Well, here I am again, facing another cold, dark night alone. I wonder if I'll ever find a place to call home? *[sighs]* At least tonight there's extra light in the sky. What a very bright star that is over there! If only I had someone to share it with.

[CAT and MOUSE enter.]

THEODORE: *[hopeful]* Oh, hello! I'm Theodore. Who are you? What are you doing?

CAT: Theodore? That's quite a name for such a little rabbit. My name is, uh, Cat and this is . . . Mouse. I guess our parents weren't too creative with names. We're just out for our nightly stroll.

THEODORE: You two are friends?

MOUSE: Oh, yes! We're ins-s-separable.

THEODORE: I thought cats were supposed to chase mice and, well, you know. . . .

CAT: Well, chasing mice used to be my favorite pastime, but I've adopted a new human lately. She's taught me a lot about being kind and loving. Even Mouse here and I have learned to get along.

THEODORE: That sounds great. I wish I had a friend.

CAT: Well, why don't you come along with us? That is, if you don't mind being seen with two animals whose names are nothing better than Cat and Mouse.

MOUSE: There's a b-b-beautiful view of the city from the top of the hill over there. Come on!

[The animals climb in place, panting as they go.]

THEODORE: Wow. It is a beautiful little town. What is the name of it?

MOUSE: The humans call it B-B-Bethlehem.

[Children's choir sings "O Little Town of Bethlehem."]

SCENE TWO: the hillside overlooking Bethlehem

CAT: If you look down there on the hillside, you can see the stable that our humans are staying in. It's right there in the rocks.

THEODORE: Your humans live in a *stable*?

MOUSE: They're just v-v-visiting. There was no other place to stay in the whole city. They l-l-looked.

THEODORE: What are their names?

MOUSE: Joseph and Mary.

CAT: *[aside]* Of course, if they'd been born in one of our families, they'd be named Boy and Girl.

THEODORE: Why are they visiting here if the only place they can stay is a stable?

MOUSE: E-Everybody in the land has to travel to the town of their b-b-birth. Joseph says it's for a senseless.

CAT: No, Joseph says it IS SENSE-LESS. They're here for a CENSUS.

THEODORE: Well, what's a cen—

AL: *[entering and loudly interrupting the last line]* Hi, everybody!

THEODORE: Who are you?

AL: Name's Al. *[aside to the audience]* That's short for Alligator! My parents weren't too creative.

MOUSE: We know just how you feel. M-m-maybe we could form a support group—

CAT: *[interrupting]* Uh, I think you're in the wrong story, buddy. I don't think there's supposed to be any alligators around here.

AL: What? Isn't this the set for *Moses Floats in the Nile for Awhile?*

CAT: Nope, this is Bethlehem.

AL: Oh, sorry! Better run—of course, I'll be running in a straight line 'cause you know alligators can't run diagonally. I didn't even know that myself—learned it watching PBS the other night! *[His voice fades as he disappears.]*

MOUSE: See ya later, Alligator!

CAT: Crazy! Now, what were we talking about?

THEODORE: You were going to tell us what *census* means.

CAT: Oh, yes. It simply means that all the people in the land are going to be counted.

MOUSE: All of them?

CAT: Yes.

THEODORE: And they're all traveling to where they were born? That does seem senseless. That's a lot of people.

MOUSE: Yes, and there's going to be w-w-one more. Mary is having a baby, right down there tonight.

CAT: Yes, our evening walk came at a *very* convenient time for everyone.

THEODORE: *[amazed at MOUSE's statement]* She is?! Down there in the stable? A baby?!

[Children's choir sings "Away in a Manger."]

SCENE THREE: the hillside overlooking Bethlehem

THEODORE: I still can't believe a human would have a baby in a stable.

[SHEEP enters quickly, plowing into the other puppets.]

SHEEP: Oh, excuse me! I was in such a hurry; I didn't see you.

MOUSE: W-Where are you going?

SHEEP: To see a king! We were all out in the fields tonight with nothing to do but sit around and chew the grass like every other night. Then, all of a sudden, the sky was as bright as day. An angel, I think they called him, was in the sky. He said, "Do not be afraid. I bring you good news of great joy that will be for all the people! Today in the town of David a Savior has been born to you; he is Christ the Lord." *[Luke 2:10, 11]* Then the whole sky was filled with angels, praising God. The humans say the baby is the Savior, the King of kings, the Prince of Peace, the Messiah they've been waiting for!

CAT: Now, *that* is an impressive name!

THEODORE: Wow, that's incredible! This night just keeps getting better! Say, isn't that interesting—two babies are being born tonight, I guess.

[Children's choir and/or congregation sing "Angels We Have Heard on High."]

SCENE FOUR: the hillside overlooking Bethlehem

SHEEP: Hey, would you like to go see the baby King?

CAT: Of course! But what about Mary and Joseph's ba—

THEODORE and **MOUSE:** *[cutting him off]* Let's go see the baby Messiah!

[Animals begin to walk in place.]

AL: *[appearing suddenly]* Hey, where are we going?

CAT: No, no! You're back in the wrong story! The NILE, you want the NILE!

AL: Oh, right! Sorry! *[He disappears quickly.]*

[Animals continue to walk in place, panting.]

MOUSE: Hey, aren't we headed for Mary and Joseph's stable?

CAT: You're right! This is the stable. Look, there's Mary and Joseph—and the new baby!

SHEEP: But *this* is where the angel told us to come! You know these people?

THEODORE: Do you mean that Mary's new baby and the baby King are the same?

CAT: Mary's baby is the Messiah? Can it be true?

[Solo: Mary Did You Know?"]

SCENE FIVE: the Christmas stable
Enter COW, HEN, ROOSTER, and GOAT, with AL in the background.

COW: Welcome, strangers, on a strange, but wonderful, night.

CAT: Tell us what has happened.

HEN: The humans have waited many years for a Savior that would save the world from sin.

SHEEP: The angels said we would find the baby here in a manger, wrapped tightly in cloths.

ROOSTER: "The people walking in darkness have seen a great light." *[Isaiah 9:2]*

CAT: So, it's true! Mary's baby is the Messiah.

GOAT: "And they will call him Immanuel—which means, 'God with us.'" *[Matthew 1:23]*

COW: "He will be called . . . Prince of Peace." *[Isaiah 9:6]*

MOUSE: So, you mean God has come to bring peace to the earth and to live with humans in the body of a little baby?

THEODORE: Immanuel—God with us. His name just keeps getting better.

CAT: Imagine, the Messiah, born in a stable, among all of us . . . a baby named the Son of God, born among a bunch of no-name sheep and goats.

[Stable animals fade to background as children's choir sings "Silent Night."]

SCENE SIX: outside the stable

THEODORE: Wow, what a night! [sighs] I suppose I'd better . . . head back.

CAT: No! Stay here with us.

MOUSE: Yes, we'd love to have you.

THEODORE: Really? I'd love to stay. I haven't felt at home like this . . . well, ever!

MOUSE: Love makes you feel that way.

THEODORE: I guess you're right. I've never seen such love. I'm so glad I was part of this night.

AL: [coming to the front] Me too!

CAT: What? You again? When are you going to stop showing up and ruining our story?!

MOUSE: You know, Cat, this night God showed His love to a lot of humans who kept trying to mess up His story too. Maybe we could let Al stay.

CAT: You're right. I guess you can stay.

AL: Great! Am I glad I kept getting mixed up in this story! I wouldn't have wanted to miss this for the world! This is amazing!

THEODORE: You can say that again!

AL: This is amazing!

CAT: He didn't really mean— [laughs and changes his tone] Oh, never mind! We are glad to have you here too. No one should miss out on this story!

[Children, puppets, and congregation sing "Joy to the World."]

BIRTHDAY CANDLES

Connie Morgan Wade

Summary: an action rhyme with props
Characters:
NARRATOR—dressed in black
5 CHILDREN—dressed in assigned solid color sweatpants and
   shirt
Props: 5 candle flame crowns (see reproducible on next page)
   sprinkled with gold glitter

NARRATOR:
   See the candles on the cake *[gesturing toward candles]*.
   Let's light them one by one.
   Their shining colors tell the news
   about God's Holy Son.

[NARRATOR pretends to light each candle.]

   BLUE:
   Blue is for His royalty,
   Jesus the King of kings.
   When He was born Heaven rejoiced,
   and angels came to sing.

   RED:
   Red is for the rosy cheeks
   on the babe so sweet.
   Mary gently kissed His head
   and toes upon His feet.

BROWN:
Brown is for the manger bed
filled with fresh cut hay.
Jesus was wrapped in strips of cloth
and in the manger lay.

WHITE:
White is for the little lambs
brought by shepherd boys.
After seeing the sweet babe,
their hearts were filled with joy.

YELLOW:
Yellow is for the brilliant star
shining in the night.
It led the wise men on
     their quest
with its guiding light.

ALL CANDLES:
We are birthday candles.
Let us cut the cake.
Jesus is God's Holy Son.
Come and celebrate!

BIRTHDAY CANDLES

POINT AND SHINE

Connie Morgan Wade

Summary: an action rhyme with props
Characters:
NARRATOR

CHILDREN

Props: stars with an arrow on one side (see reproducible on next page) and glitter glued on the other side; hot glue each star onto a tongue depressor

NARRATOR:
What is a star's job?
What does it do?
What is a star's job?
I really wish I knew!

CHILDREN:
Point [turn arrow side of star out]
and shine [turn glitter side out].
Point and shine.
All throughout the night,
pointing all to Jesus,
bringing joy and light.

NARRATOR:
Oh, stars are very beautiful.
Yes, stars are very bold.
Oh, stars are very beautiful,
all silvery and gold.

CHILDREN:

Point *[turn arrow side of star out]*
and shine *[turn glitter side out].*
Point and shine.
All throughout the night,
pointing all to Jesus,
bringing joy and light.

NARRATOR:

What is a star's job?
What does it do?
Points the way to Jesus
and lets God's love shine
through.

CHILDREN:

Point *[turn arrow side of star out]*
and shine *[turn glitter side out].*
Point and shine.
All throughout the night,
pointing all to Jesus,
bringing joy and light.

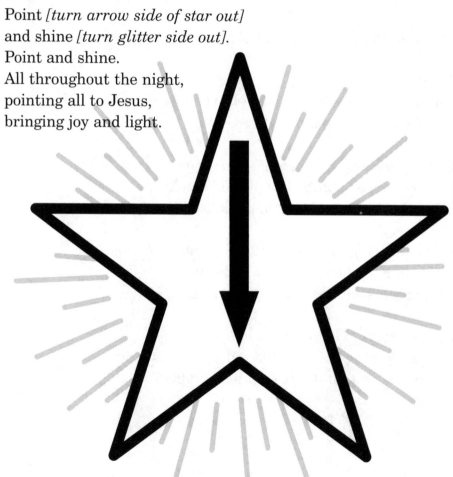

POINT AND SHINE

CHRISTMAS CANDY

Connie Morgan Wade

Summary: action rhyme with prop
Prop: candy cane (see reproducible on next page); color as
needed

All children enter, each one holding a cardstock candy cane.

ALL:
Oh, candy cane, sweet taste of Christmas,
you show to all the story of Jesus.

GIRLS: *[holding up canes with curve on top]*
Its very shape is both straight and crooked,
like a shepherd staff long and hooked.

BOYS: *[holding up canes with the curve on bottom]*
It makes a *J* when the curve is down.
Jesus begins with that letter and sound.

GIRLS: *[point to white stripe and then red]*
The candy cane is white and red.
It reminds us that Jesus suffered and bled.

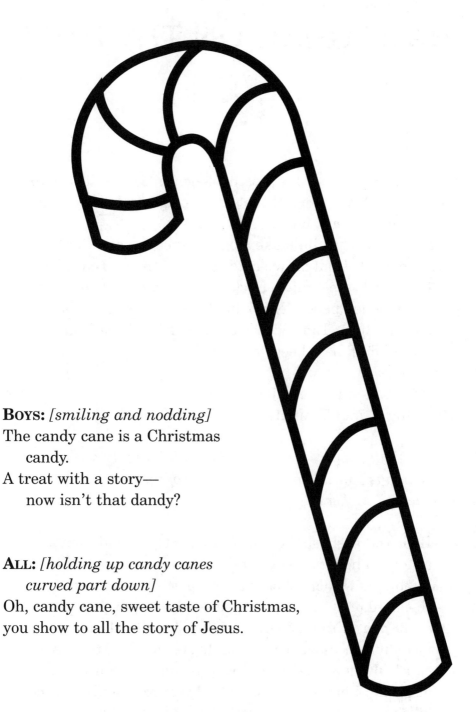

BOYS: [*smiling and nodding*]
The candy cane is a Christmas candy.
A treat with a story—
    now isn't that dandy?

ALL: [*holding up candy canes curved part down*]
Oh, candy cane, sweet taste of Christmas,
you show to all the story of Jesus.

CHRISTMAS CANDY

HALLELUJAH ON THE HILL!

Lori Morrison

Summary: This skit for preschool-age children will acquaint them with the story of the angel appearing to shepherds to announce Jesus' birth.
Props: Let each child make a pair of sheep's ears. Cut 2" wide bands from brown card stock, fit them to each child's head, and staple into a circle. Give each child two black construction paper "ears" and help children glue cotton balls to them. Tape or staple the ears to the band and let the children be "sheep" for the skit.
Characters:
HALLELUJAH—an angel puppet
Running Time: 5 minutes

HALLELUJAH appears from behind a "hill" singing several "hallelujahs" until she becomes aware of the sheep and shepherds (teachers).

Hello there, sheep. My name is Hallelujah, and I am an angel. An honest-to-goodness, sent-by-God angel. Now I know that where there are sheep, there is sure to be a shepherd or two. So, sheep, do you have a shepherd? *[pause for response]* You do! Great. Hello, shepherds! I have an incredible message for you all. Is everybody sitting? Are you sure? OK, don't be afraid, even though I am rather awe-inspiring! I have great news. God sent me way out in these hills to tell you about a baby. Now, this isn't just any baby.

This is a special baby. Do you know why? *[pause for response]* That's right. This baby is God's Son. He was born in a stable—that's another name for a stinky old barn. Yep, He was born where cows, donkeys, and sheep live. Sheep, just like you. Now why would God's Son be born in a stinky barn? Do you think maybe His parents should have gone to the hospital? No, they couldn't, because back when baby Jesus was born, they didn't have hospitals like you do today.

Now when Mary and Joseph—you know, the baby's mom and dad—well, when they traveled to a town called Bethlehem, they went to an inn. An inn is like a hotel. Have you ever stayed in a hotel? *[pause for response]* But there were so many people in the inn that there was no room for them. So, they went to a stable and that is where Jesus was born. Then, God sent an angel, HALLELUJAH, that's me, to tell the shepherds about baby Jesus. God wants all His creation to tell others about Jesus. Can you sheep talk? Let me hear you! *[pause for response]*

Will you tell your parents, grandparents, brothers, sisters, friends, family, and neighbors about Jesus? *[pause for response]* Tell them He is the reason we celebrate Christmas. And I'd better go tell some more people myself. Good-bye!

[After skit, give children cookies or graham crackers and help them spread icing on them. Then let children add mini-marshmallows to look like sheep's wool.]

'TWAS THE WEEK BEFORE CHRISTMAS

Lori Morrison

'Twas the week before Christmas and all through the land
holiday preparations were quite out of hand.
Cookies were baking and presents were bought.
Kids tried to be good or at least not get caught.

Families were doing what families do best—
running around, never stopping to rest
as they trimmed all their trees and put up decorations,
hoping to meet all their friends' expectations.

"We must have some reindeer!" they'd say with a shout
as they rustled and bustled and hustled about.
They'd haul out their Santas and drag out some elves.
They'd put plastic holly on top of their shelves.
They'd sing all the carols—the words they still knew.
They'd go to a holiday party or two.
And then in the midst of this chaos and stress,
Christmas had started to be quite a mess
and a bother, a nuisance, a worry, a chore—
yes, Christmas was getting to be quite a bore.
"How in the world did this happen?" they wondered.
Where had they gone wrong? Where had they blundered?
When had they lost touch with goodwill, peace on earth?
It was when they forgot about Jesus' birth.
He came in a stable and not to the mall.
He came as a servant and Savior for all.
God so loved the world that He sent us His Son.
So let's not forget Jesus because He is the One
who makes Christmas holy, blessed, and right.
Happy Jesus to all and to all a good night.

JESUS' BIRTH
Dolores Steger

When fireplaces glow with embers
in the coldness of Decembers,
warmth descends upon the earth
as peace, love, hope in Jesus' birth.

CHRISTMAS MORN
Dolores Steger

On Christmas Eve in bed I'll be.
I'll close my eyes and there I'll see
a vision—the nativity.

The stars glow in the heavens where
they shine on stable cold and bare.
A babe rests, tender, sleeping there.

An angel band, their trumpets play
while shepherds come to honor, pray,
and wise men bring their gifts array.

I wake on Christmas morn to find
the scene still in my heart and mind
and praise the Child sent to mankind.

THE STAR
Karen Leet

Summary: A performance poem that may be read or recited as a group or with individual assigned parts. Costumes and motions may be added.

Star in the sky
bright to see,
lighting the night,
leading me.

I follow the star
to find a king.
In the distance
angels sing.

I find a stable
with cattle and hay—
I kneel by a manger
and start to pray.

Star in the sky
bright to see,
lighting the night,
leading me
to the babe who came
to make me free.

FAMILY CHRISTMAS
Charlotte Adelsperger

I'll always remember Christmas
with excitement in the air.
Loved ones all together,
and God's great love was there.

SLEEP, LITTLE BABY
Dolores Steger

Sleep, little baby, sleep the night through.
Heavenly angels keep watch over You.
Mary and Joseph are guarding You too.
Sleep, little baby, sleep the night through.

Sleep, little baby, sleep while You may.
While those around You rejoice as they pray.
Knowing that You are the light and the way,
Sleep, little baby,
  and happy birthday.

CHRISTMAS JOY, CHRISTMAS CHEER

Dolores Steger

Christmas joy, Christmas cheer.
It comes at this time each year.
It brings smiles to all we meet.
It brings carols, soft and sweet.
It brings trees to decorate.
It brings nights to stay up late.
It brings Jesus and His birth.
It brings hope of peace on earth.
Christmas joy and Christmas cheer.
May it last throughout the year.

REALMS OF JOY

Charlotte Adelsperger

Oh, the excitement
of a toddler's Christmas!
Little hands tear open crackling paper,
enveloping presents of clothes and toys.
What joy—feeling so loved!

Oh, the excitement
of a new believer's Christmas!
Eager hands open printed pages,
releasing God's living Word.
What joy—feeling so loved!

BUSY, BUSY CHRISTMAS
Karen Leet

Summary: This is a performance poem that may be read or recited as a group or with individual assigned parts. Costumes and motions may be added.

Hurry here, hurry there,
Hurry, hurry everywhere.
Christmas is coming, coming fast.
Put up the tree!
Hang the lights!
Bake more cookies!
Buy some presents!
Wrap them nicely!
Sing some carols!
Watch Christmas movies!
So much to do!

Hurry here, hurry there,
Hurry, hurry everywhere.
Rush and fuss. So much to do!
Hurry here, hurry there,
Hurry, hurry everywhere.
Wait a moment. Be still and see
all that Christmas is meant to be.
Stop the hurry! Stop the rush!
Shh, wait a moment. Shh, hush.
Listen for the sound of angels singing—
feel the joy baby Jesus is bringing.

I HAVE A CHRISTMAS MESSAGE
Dixie Phillips

Costumes: costumes for angel, shepherd, and wise man

Three children enter.

ANGEL:
I have a Christmas message of joy.
Such good news! It's a baby boy!

SHEPHERD:
I have a Christmas message too.
He was born for me and born for you.
[points to congregation]

WISE MAN:
I have a Christmas message to share.
God's gift is the grandest gift anywhere.